WORLD WAR I

From the *Lusitania* to Versailles

Zachary Kent

Enslow Publishers, Inc.
40 Industrial Road
Box 398
Berkeley Heights, NJ 07922
USA

http://www.enslow.com

"This war, like the next war, is a war to end war."
—David Lloyd George, British prime minister from 1916 to 1922

Original edition published as *World War I: "The War to End Wars"* in 1994.

Library of Congress Cataloging-in-Publication Data

Kent, Zachary.
  World War I : from the Lusitania to Versailles / Zachary Kent.
     p. cm. — (The United States at war)
  Summary: "Examines World War I, including the causes of the war, the important leaders and battles, America's involvement in the war, the home front, and the Allied victory"—Provided by publisher.
  Includes bibliographical references and index.
  ISBN 978-0-7660-3641-3
  1. World War, 1914–1918—United States—Juvenile literature. 2. World War, 1914–1918—Juvenile literature. I. Title. II. Title: World War One.
  D522.7.K34 2011
  940.3—dc22
                              2010023908

Printed in the United States of America

112010 Lake Book Manufacturing, Inc., Melrose Park, IL

10 9 8 7 6 5 4 3 2 1

To Our Readers: We have done our best to make sure all Internet addresses in this book were active and appropriate when we went to press. However, the author and the publisher have no control over and assume no liability for the material available on those Internet sites or on other Web sites they may link to. Any comments or suggestions can be sent by e-mail to comments@enslow.com or to the address on the back cover.

♻ Enslow Publishers, Inc., is committed to printing our books on recycled paper. The paper in every book contains 10% to 30% post-consumer waste (PCW). The cover board on the outside of each book contains 100% PCW. Our goal is to do our part to help young people and the environment too!

Illustration Credits: Associated Press, pp. 17, 45, 70, 84; Domenick D'Andrea, pp. 94–95; Enslow Publishers, Inc., pp. 19, 117; The Granger Collection, New York, pp. 13, 28, 35, 64, 81, 107, 112, 115; John D. Shaw, p. 99; Library of Congress, pp. 1, 6, 10, 14, 31, 39, 55, 57, 77; © Military and Historical Image Bank, p. 23; National Archives and Records Administration, pp. 4–5, 46, 51, 52, 60, 62, 90, 103, 110; Official White House photo by Pete Souza, p. 119; Rue des Archives / The Granger Collection, New York, pp. 8, 37, 86; Texas Military Forces Museum, Camp Mabry, Austin, Texas, p. 105; Courtesy of William S. Phillips, pp. 68, 88.

Cover Illustration: Library of Congress (U.S. Marine recruitment poster from World War I).

CONTENTS

FOREWORD

At a country auction in upstate New York many years ago, I bought a handsome pair of brass binoculars. They had belonged to a man named G. G. Volkmar. Etched on the brass were the words *U.S. Navy.* Included with the binoculars was a very interesting letter dated May 9, 1918:

> Dear Sir:
>
> Your prompt and patriotic response to the NAVY's call for binoculars . . . is most appreciated. The glasses will be very useful in the prosecution of Naval Operations until victory is won. . . . On behalf of the NAVY, I wish to thank you most heartily.
>
> Very respectfully,
>
> Franklin D. Roosevelt
> Assistant Secretary of the Navy

In 1914, war erupted across Europe. The Allied nations of France, Great Britain, and Russia battled against the Central Powers of Germany,

Austria-Hungary, and Turkey in what became known as the Great War. When the United States entered the fight on the side of the Allies in 1917, every loyal American citizen wished to pitch in. Mr. Volkmar gladly loaned his binoculars to America's war effort.

When I look at that pair of binoculars now resting on my living-room table, I am reminded of that time. When World War I ended in 1918, 116,000 American soldiers had died of wounds and disease. These men represented only a small number among the millions who perished in World War I. It was a senseless war and a brutal war, more horrible than anyone could have imagined. When it joined the fight, the United States found a national pride that propelled it to international greatness. But in the process, America lost its sense of innocence.

THE SINKING OF THE *LUSITANIA*

NOTICE! TRAVELLERS INTENDING TO EMBARK ON THE ATLANTIC VOYAGE ARE REMINDED THAT A STATE OF WAR EXISTS BETWEEN GERMANY AND HER ALLIES AND GREAT BRITAIN AND HER ALLIES; THAT THE ZONE OF WAR INCLUDES THE WATERS ADJACENT TO THE BRITISH ISLES.

—From a warning printed in the *New York Times* by the Imperial German Embassy, May 1, 1915

A long, black German submarine lurked unseen beneath the ocean's surface. Several miles off the southern coast of Ireland, Captain Walther Schwieger raised the periscope of U-boat 20. Peering through the eyepiece, he could hardly believe what he saw. Steaming along some seven hundred yards away was the great British passenger liner *Lusitania*. The *Lusitania*, the fastest ship on the Atlantic Ocean, weighed 31,550 tons and was 790 feet in length. In Germany's war against Great Britain, the sinking of such a target would be a tremendous victory. At just after two o'clock on the afternoon of May 7, 1915, Schwieger ordered, "Fire one!" In the torpedo room, a sailor pulled a firing lever. A fierce hissing swept through the submarine as high-pressure air blasted the torpedo out of its tube.

Aboard the *Lusitania*, passenger Oliver Bernard caught sight of something strange as he gazed out at the bright blue sea. "What is that streak in the water?" he wondered. "It's spreading. It's coming closer."[1] A ship's lookout suddenly noticed the white wake and shouted, "Torpedo coming on the starboard side!" Within seconds, the torpedo crashed into the liner's hull. The explosion sounded like "a million-ton hammer" hitting a giant steel drum, passenger Michael Byrne remembered. It is not clear whether the second explosion that quickly followed was caused by a

This advertisement from the New York Herald *announced the sailing of the* Lusitania *from New York to Liverpool, England, on May 1, 1915. At the bottom of the ad, there is a notice about the danger of traveling on the Atlantic because of the war between Germany and England.*

cargo of ammunition stowed aboard the *Lusitania* or by an exploding boiler. The second explosion rocked the ship. On the starboard side, deck planks, lifeboats, coal dust, and water flew upward. In the dining saloon, fearful first-class passengers scattered away from their tables as the glass from shattered windows showered them. Elsewhere, the force of the blast knocked people to the floor. Flames and smoke poured into some staterooms and through corridors.

Aboard the German U-20, Captain Schwieger stared through his periscope. "Shot hits starboard side right behind bridge," he noted in his log. "A . . . heavy detonation follows with a very strong explosion cloud."[2]

Already, the *Lusitania* was tilting to starboard and settling deeper into the water. From below, the crew tumbled out onto the boat deck. "Boat stations!" Captain William Turner soon ordered. The crewmen prepared to lower the lifeboats. Alarmed passengers streamed up the stairways or wandered about in confusion. Passengers carrying babies and life jackets struggled to reach the deck. Many rushed upstairs shirtless or shoeless. Cursing and shrieking, the terrified crowd pressed up against the deck rails. Without engine power, the ship drifted. Tons of seawater poured in through open lower-deck portholes. Passengers trapped inside the ship's electric elevator screamed for help as the water slowly rose about their feet.

the cold sea. On the rescue boats, the survivors huddled under blankets and sipped hot tea as they were brought back to land. The passengers and crew of the *Lusitania* had numbered 1,959. Altogether, 1,198 perished in the disaster, including 270 women and 94 children.

Americans gasped when they heard the news. "American citizens are among the victims," the *New York Tribune* soon exclaimed. There had been 197 Americans on board, and 128 of them had lost their lives.

Many newspapers published a heartbreaking family photograph. It showed Mrs. Paul Crompton of Philadelphia and her six children, all of whom were lost. The brave millionaire Alfred Vanderbilt and other well-known Americans also had drowned. The New York *American* called the German torpedo attack a "deed of wholesale murder." Since 1914, war had raged across Europe. But most Americans bitterly condemned this new type of submarine warfare against defenseless ships. The *New York Times* declared: "From our Department of State there must go to the Imperial Government at Berlin a demand that the Germans shall no longer make war like savages drunk with blood." Colonel Edward M. House, a close adviser to U.S. president Woodrow Wilson, predicted, "We shall be at war with Germany within a month."[3]

But Wilson wished to keep America neutral and out of the war at all costs. In a speech in

Philadelphia three days after the sinking, Wilson proclaimed: "There is such a thing as a man being too proud to fight. There is such a thing as a nation being so right that it does not need to convince others by force that it is right."[4]

In this illustration, passengers and crew from the Lusitania *scramble to get into lifeboats as the large ship sinks in the Atlantic.*

Many Americans disagreed. The *New York Times* declared that "this utterance of the President does not respond to the feeling of the people." The *New York World* insisted: "We have a pride that will make us fight." The sympathies of the American people had been split between Britain and Germany until the "Lusitania Massacre." After the ship's sinking, Americans turned their outrage toward Germany. Many began preparing for a war. Manufacturers worked with more energy to supply the Allies. Young men flocked to summer military camps to learn how to be soldiers. Two more years would pass before the United States declared war on Germany. But the sinking of the *Lusitania* made many Americans eager to join the fight.

2

THE WORLD AT WAR

FOR ALL WE HAVE AND ARE,
FOR ALL OUR CHILDREN'S FATE,
STAND UP AND MEET THE WAR.
THE HUN IS AT THE GATE!

—From the poem "For All We Have and Are"
by British author Rudyard Kipling

In the first fateful days of August 1914, when World War I was beginning, no one could guess that before its end the whole world would be drawn into conflict. Thrones would topple, empires would disappear, and countries would vanish. The world would never be the same again.

The Fatal Shots

Archduke Franz Ferdinand and his wife, Sophie, were being driven in an open automobile through the streets of Sarajevo in Bosnia on June 28, 1914. The fifty-one-year-old archduke, heir to the Hapsburg Empire of Austria-Hungary, was scheduled to attend a review of Austrian troops. The people of Bosnia were Serbs and Croats. Many of them resented being part of the Hapsburg Empire instead of Serbia, their national state. Several Serbian university students stood in the crowd along the parade route. They planned to use this opportunity to assassinate the hated archduke.

One plotter heaved a bomb at the passing automobile. It landed in the street and exploded, spraying fragments in all directions. The startled archduke remained unhurt. Angrily, he ordered the chauffeur to drive straight out of town. The chauffeur, however, took a wrong turn, then stopped the car and reversed. In the roadside crowd, Gavrilo Princip, another of the assassins, jumped onto the running board. He drew a pistol and fired twice. One bullet struck Ferdinand in the neck. The other hit Sophie in the abdomen. Both died almost immediately.

The archduke's murder shocked Europeans and set off a deadly chain reaction. At the start of the 1900s, three cousins, all grandsons of Great Britain's Queen Victoria, ruled three of Europe's largest nations. Wilhelm II sat on the throne as kaiser of Germany, Nicholas II ruled as absolute czar of Russia, and George V wore the crown of king of Great Britain. Since 1870, when Germany first became a united nation, its leaders had desired greater world power. Great Britain and France possessed colonies throughout the world. Germany wished to establish colonies, too. During the next forty years, Germany built up a navy and an army and factories to support them. German Navy yards rushed to build ships.

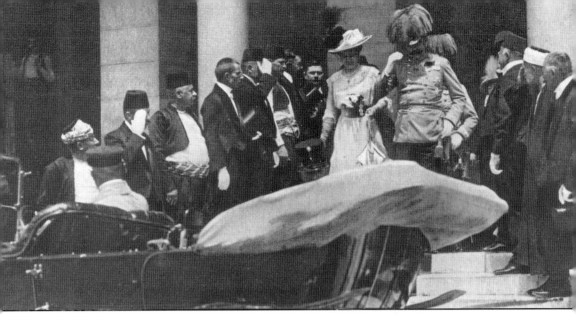

Archduke Franz Ferdinand and his wife walk toward an open car in Sarajevo, Bosnia, on June 28, 1914. The couple were assassinated while being driven through the city streets.

The kaiser, on horseback, proudly reviewed new German infantry regiments, and German munitions factories, such as the giant Krupp works, manufactured tons of heavy cannons, artillery, and rifles.

These German efforts to gain increased power worried many Europeans. The assassination of Archduke Ferdinand provided the spark that would touch off a war. Arnold Whitridge, a young American student traveling in Europe in 1914, realized that

> [a]fter Archduke Franz Ferdinand was assassinated, you could see the tensions building up everywhere—one thing just seemed to follow another. . . . There hadn't been a major war in Europe for so many years, and everyone seemed to clamor for one.[1]

The Age of Alliances

During the previous twenty years, Europe had formed itself into a confused tangle of political and military alliances, in which one nation pledged to support another. Allied together, the governments of Austria-Hungary and Germany thought they had become very powerful. Archduke Franz Ferdinand's death put the strength of Europe's various alliances to the test.

"Serbia must learn to fear us again," declared Austrian diplomat Wilhelm Ritter von Storck after Ferdinand's assassination. Kaiser Wilhelm II of Germany also advised his Austrian allies to take a strong line. On July 23, the Austro-Hungarian government sent a list of vengeful legal demands to Serbia designed to give Austria-Hungary greater power over that country. When the Serbs failed to meet all these demands, Austria-Hungary declared war on Serbia on July 28, 1914.

Austria-Hungary had Germany as an ally, but Serbia had Russia. On July 30, Czar Nicholas II ordered Russia's Army to prepare for war. German diplomats demanded that Russia halt its plans at once. The Russians refused, and on August 1, 1914, Germany declared war on Russia. Two days later, Germany declared war on France, another Russian ally. World War I began because statesmen foolishly thought they could bully one another with threats.

Prior to World War I, the continent of Europe was divided by many political and military alliances. The borders of nations would change dramatically by war's end. This is a map of Europe in 1914.

On August 2, Germany demanded free passage through Belgium in order to attack France. The Belgians refused, and this refusal brought Belgium's ally Great Britain into the war. Germany was already wheeling 1.5 million soldiers into line toward France. Another 500,000 were mobilized to face eastward toward Russia. Across Europe, more than 6 million soldiers were getting marching orders. Troop trains with whistles screaming rolled out of railroad stations. People crowded the streets in every capital, excitedly yelling "to Paris" or "to Berlin."

The Western Front

"You will be home before the leaves have fallen from the trees," Kaiser Wilhelm told his departing troops. Germany's military Schlieffen Plan called for the German Army to march through the Low Countries of Belgium and Luxembourg and invade France from the weakly defended north. A young lieutenant commanded the lead company of the German 69th Infantry Regiment that crossed the Luxembourg border at 7:00 P.M. on August 1, 1914, and captured the railway station at the village of Ulflingen. Within twenty-four hours, Luxembourg was fully occupied. German general Erich Ludendorff captured the key Belgian city of Liege by battering it to pieces with heavy howitzer fire during a ten-day siege. Elsewhere, the German advance was even more swift and brutal.

"Frightened civilians lined the streets," German lieutenant Fritz Nagel remembered, "hands held high as a sign of surrender. Bedsheets hung out of windows for the same purpose. To see those frightened men, women, and children was a really terrible sight."

British newspapers printed horror stories of the German march through Belgium. Articles told of Belgian girls and women tortured and murdered and of children stabbed with bayonets and trampled beneath the hooves of German cavalry horses. Mobs of panicked Belgians crowded the dusty roads, fleeing the German advance. The British compared the Germans to the hordes of Huns who had swarmed through Europe in the Middle Ages.

• • • • • • • • • • • • • • • • • • •

"To see those frightened men, women, and children was a really terrible sight."

• • • • • • • • • • • • • • • • • • •

The Third and Fourth armies of France counterattacked eastward from the province of Lorraine on August 14. The offensive shattered when it came up against strong fortifications at the German border. At the same time, Sir John French led 100,000 British soldiers across the English Channel and took up a position near the Belgian border at Mons, France. On August 22, a British pilot reported seeing field gray German columns rolling toward the twenty-seven-mile British front.

At Mons on August 23, 1914, two British divisions of 35,000 men held off four German army corps of more than 160,000 men. British rifle fire cut down the charging Germans in rows. British corporal W. Holbrook recalled, "You'd see a lot of them coming in a mass . . . and you just let them have it. They kept retreating, and then coming forward, and then retreating again." Heavily outnumbered, by day's end, the British had to retreat. "The position was hopeless," British lieutenant K.F.B. Tower later declared. "We darted off under a hail of fire and I don't know how on earth we got away."[2]

After knocking the British out of his path, commanding German general Helmuth von Moltke ordered a major change in the Schlieffen Plan. Now the Germans turned southwest and marched toward Paris. On September 2, a German biplane dropped propaganda leaflets over Paris with the message: "There is nothing you can do but surrender." As the Germans crossed the Marne River, fifty miles from Paris, French general Joseph Joffre called for a desperate French counterattack. "Soldiers of France," he sternly commanded, "we are attacking. Advance as long as you can. When you can no longer advance, hold your position. When you can no longer hold it, die."

Belgian troops fight off a German advance in 1914. The German march through Belgium was swift and brutal.

For seven days, the Germans and the French recklessly attacked one another all along the Western Front. On the huge battlefield of the Marne, both sides fell in bloody waves. When the French weakened at one point along the line on September 8, French general Joseph Gallieni collected some 1,200 taxicabs in Paris and rushed in several thousand reinforcements to save the position. Known as the "Miracle of the Marne," this movement helped turn the tide against the Germans. On September 14, the exhausted Germans pulled back to the Aisne River. They scratched holes in the ground and set up machine guns. The enemy armies now glared at one another from the safety of opposing networks of defensive ditches. Trench warfare had begun. The war of movement had ended.

The Eastern Front

In August 1914, only 135,000 soldiers defended Germany's eastern border in Prussia. With surprising speed, 650,000 Russian soldiers, commanded by Grand Duke Nicholas, the uncle of the czar, marched against that line. At Gumbinnen on August 20, the Russians overwhelmed the enemy and threatened to overrun East Prussia (present-day Poland). In this German emergency, sixty-seven-year-old General Paul von Hindenburg was brought out of retirement and named new commander of the German Eighth Army.

On August 29, the Germans attacked around the city of Tannenberg in East Prussia along a sixty-mile front. The Masurian Lakes created a wide gap between two major Russian armies. The German soldiers first attacked one army and then the other. In four days, 90,000 Russian prisoners were taken. Broken Russian divisions fell back in disorder. The Battle of Tannenberg cleared German territory and made Hindenburg a German national hero.

In the fall of 1914, the Germans pushed east into Poland. On December 6, the Germans captured the city of Lodz. In March 1915, the Tenth Russian Army was destroyed in the Polish forest of Augustow. The whole Russian Army was poorly trained and equipped. In battle, many unarmed troops had to snatch rifles from the hands of their dead comrades. As their battle line broke apart, the Russians abandoned most of Poland. On August 5, the Russians evacuated the city of Warsaw in a general retreat. By the end of August 1915, the Russians had lost 750,000 men as prisoners alone and more territory than the whole of France. German general Erich Ludendorff commented, "We had taken a great step toward Russia's overthrow."

• • • • • • • • • • • • • • • • • • •

By the end of August 1915, the Russians had lost 750,000 men as prisoners alone and more territory than the whole of France.

• • • • • • • • • • • • • • • • • • •

Farther south in Galicia, in Austria-Hungary, vast hordes of Russians and Serbs smashed an Austrian Army. By November 1914, the Russians reached the Carpathian Mountains leading into Hungary. In the spring of 1915, the Germans aided the Austrians in a furious counterattack. On May 2, they captured the city of Tarnow and continued attacking the Russians along a 250-mile front, capturing 150,000 prisoners.

Faced with disaster, Czar Nicholas II dismissed his uncle as the Russian army's commander-in-chief. On September 5, 1915, the czar announced, "Today I have taken supreme command of all forces of the sea and land armies operating in

German soldiers wearing gas masks stand in their trench in this painting made in 1917. Chemical weapons caused thousands of casualties during the war.

The gasping, the gasping! And . . . your eyes were stinging as well. You couldn't stop to help anybody, even if he was your brother."

Later, phosgene gas proved twice as deadly as chlorine. Soon, all troops were wearing protective gas masks. Over the course of the war, gas caused more than 79,000 deaths.

At the war's start, every army possessed a few airplanes that were used for the purpose transports discharging their troops into destroyers, which then darted towards the shore to discharge the men into rowing boats. Shells were bursting around and over the vessels and boats and we could hear the crackling of machine guns and rifles.

"There were lines of men clinging like cockroaches under the cliffs," recalled Irish captain Aubrey Herbert. "The only thing to be done was to dig in as soon as possible, but a good many men were shot while they were doing this." The British troops were pinned down on the rocky shore, unable to reach the top of the hills and move into open country. There was no shade. Everything, even water, had to be landed at night. New Zealander private Leonard Hart declared:

> During these days our losses had been very heavy and a number of our men had been taken bad with . . . fever. The smell of the bodies was becoming intolerable and the flies swarmed in the millions. When a man was killed in the trenches all that could be done was to throw him up on the parapet and leave him until we could spare time at night to bury him.[5]

On August 6, 1915, the British landed five more divisions on Gallipoli, at Anzac Bay and at Sulva Bay. Though they surprised the Turks, the British failed to press their advantage. Finally, after eight months of stalemate, the British evacuated the peninsula in January 1916. At Gallipoli, they had lost 250,000 men, including those killed, wounded, and missing. The Turks also suffered some 250,000 casualties.

The Battle of Jutland was the only major engagement of the British and German fleets during the war. The Imperial German Navy challenged the British Royal Navy for control of the seas. Sailors fought the battle on May 31, 1916, about sixty miles west of the Danish coast of Jutland. Commanded by Admiral Sir John Jellicoe, the British had twenty-eight dreadnoughts (battleships), nine battle cruisers, and assorted other ships. The Germans, led by Admiral Reinhard Scheer, had twenty-two dreadnoughts and five battle cruisers, among its fleet. In all, 250 vessels steamed into combat. Cannon fire flashed across the sea beginning at 6 P.M. The fighting ended late in the night, when the Germans, under the cover of darkness and fog, made their escape. The British lost three battle cruisers, three armored cruisers, and eight destroyers. German losses included the battle cruiser *Lutzow*, the battleship *Pommern*, four light cruisers, and four destroyers. The Battle of Jutland forced the German fleet to remain inside its harbors for the rest of the war. As a result, submarines became the German navy's greatest weapon.

In the Middle East, Turkey kept the British occupied. The British wished to protect the Suez Canal in Egypt and their oil wells in Persia (present-day Iran). In time, 600,000 British

This engraving depicts the Battle of Jutland on May 31, 1916, the only major naval battle between the British and German fleets during the war.

soldiers were engaged in Mesopotamia (present-day Iraq) and 500,000 more in Palestine.

In 1916, British colonel T. E. Lawrence helped Arab forces under Sheik Faisal al Husein revolt against the Turks on the Arabian Peninsula (present-day Saudi Arabia). Dressed in Arab clothes, "Lawrence of Arabia" led attacks against the Turkish Hejaz railroad and urged the Arab forces under Faisal to cooperate with the British general Sir Edmund Allenby.

"I'd like you to take Jerusalem as a Christmas present for the nation," British prime minister David Lloyd George told General Allenby in June 1917. Allenby obliged. After capturing Beersheba, the British lay siege to Jerusalem. The city surrendered on December 9. By late 1918,

Colonel Lawrence and General Allenby were operating together, pushing north on parallel routes through the Holy Land toward the city of Damascus. Earlier, in Mesopotamia, 400,000 British soldiers commanded by General Sir Stanley Maude had marched up the Tigris River and captured Baghdad in March 1917.

They Shall Not Pass

"The German Army, when it moves to attack, stops for no obstacle," the kaiser's son Crown Prince Rupprecht announced on the Western Front at the start of 1916. General Erich von Falkenhayn of Germany wished to destroy the will of France to fight. He chose the famous fortress at Verdun, on the Meuse River in northern France, as the place to rob the French of their pride. The German buildup of nearly a thousand heavy guns included thirteen 420-millimeter mortars (called "Big Berthas") that threw one-ton projectiles. On February 21, 1916, across a six-mile front, the Germans threw one million shells into the forts and trenches of Verdun. The shells rained down at the rate of 100,000 an hour.

Crown Prince Rupprecht's Fifth German Army led the assault that followed. The French defenses east of the Meuse River began to sag. French marshal Henri Philippe Pétain took command at Verdun and solemnly vowed, "They shall not pass." The French possessed a single

French soldiers under attack during the Battle of Verdun. Both the French and German armies lost hundreds of thousands of soldiers during this battle.

road leading to the front. Trucks carried 27,000 tons of ammunition and supplies and 190,000 reinforcements along this crucial road, called "The Sacred Way."

The fighting at Verdun was gruesome. A French lieutenant wrote: "What scenes of horror and carnage! . . . Hell cannot be so terrible." American ambulance driver Robert Lowell Moore later declared, "The poor devils, we'd just load them in the ambulance and head for the hospital, over and over again." The French held Verdun, but, by the end of June, they had lost some 500,000 soldiers, and the Germans had lost more than 400,000.

Just as the fighting ended at Verdun, it flared up between the British and the Germans along the Somme River farther north in the province of Picardy. The Battle of the Somme opened with five days of heavy British bombardment on an eighteen-mile front. Of the shelling, British captain R. J. Trousdell remembered, "Thickly timbered woods were reduced to a few gaunt and splintered trunks. . . . Villages disappeared as though they had never been."

On July 1, 1916, thirteen British divisions, about 200,000 men, went forward together. Climbing "over the top" of their trenches, the troops started across No-Man's-Land. The Germans swiftly emerged from their dugouts and manned their machine guns. The first British line went into a steady spray of bullets. It faltered and fell, a second followed it, a third, and then a fourth, all to no avail. "We never got anywhere near the Germans," British corporal W. H. Shaw exclaimed. "Never got anywhere near them. . . . The machine-guns . . . were mowing the top of the trenches. You daren't put your finger up. The men were just falling back in the trenches."[6] On that gory July day, 20,000 British soldiers died, the heaviest loss suffered in a single day by any army in World War I.

British general Sir Douglas Haig continued the hopeless fight day after day. During one attack, three divisions of cavalry made a charge. With bugles blowing and lances glittering, men and horses were mowed down as the German machine guns opened fire. Tragically, these mounted troops learned there was no place for cavalry in modern trench warfare.

No-Man's-Land in Flander's Fields, France. During the Battle of the Somme, British soldiers suffered devastating casualties as they marched across No-Man's-Land while German soldiers picked them off with machine-gun fire.

In desperation, Haig tried a new weapon: the tank. Hidden under canvas during its secret development, this machine was called a "water carrier" or "water tank," soon shortened to "tank." Tank designers enclosed caterpillar tractors inside fully armored cabins.

On September 15, 1916, Haig threw forty-two of them into his attack. British private Charles Cole watched one of the strange machines:

> Eventually, the tank got going and went past us. The Germans ran for their lives—couldn't make out what was firing at them. . . . The tank went

on, knocked brick walls, houses down, did what it was supposed to have done—but too late! We lost thousands and thousands. . . .

Haig finally called off the fighting on November 18, 1916. The Somme campaign was a dreadful failure. The British had advanced no more than five miles, and some 420,000 men had been killed or wounded.

The Hindenburg Line

New men and new methods set the scene on the Western Front for 1917. British Lord Kitchener drowned at sea when the warship *Hampshire* struck a mine and sank off the Orkney Islands on June 5, 1916. General Sir William Robertson took over as supreme director of strategy for the British. When Joseph Joffre was named marshal of France, General Robert Nivelle became French commander of the Western Front. In August 1916, Hindenburg took over in the West as chief of the German general staff with General Erich Ludendorff as first quartermaster general.

Ludendorff soon decided to simplify the German line. Through the winter of 1916–1917, the Germans prepared a new "Hindenburg Line," carefully chosen for its advantages. Dugouts were constructed and equipped. Concrete positions were built for machine guns. Falling back into this line, Ludendorff could successfully defend his territory with fewer soldiers.

The British began 1917 with an attack at Arras, France, on April 9. British rifleman Ralph Langley described the scene:

> It went on snowing all the time we were advancing. Off we went, and just as we got up to the wire the Germans got me through the leg with a bullet. A rifle bullet. You could see them firing at us. And there were machine-guns going too. . . .
> I don't know what the Generals wanted to do that attack for, because it was murder.

The fight cost 150,000 British casualties and gained little.

The French also staged an attack that spring. "We will win it all," General Nivelle insisted, "within twenty-four to forty-eight hours."[7]

• • • • • • • • • • • • • • • • • •

"I don't know what the Generals wanted to do that attack for, because it was murder."

• • • • • • • • • • • • • • • • • •

The "Nivelle system," of which he was so proud, called for a swift concentration of troops across the Aisne River. On April 16, Nivelle attacked with three entire French armies, totaling some 1.2 million men. The guns thundered. The whistles blew. French infantry masses slogged forward in a storm of rain and snow that turned the ground to mud. German artillery showered death on their heads. By evening, the French had gained six hundred yards, not the six miles Nivelle had promised. The trenches and concrete shelters of the Hindenburg Line still frowned in the distance.

Nivelle continued the hopeless attack for another ten days. The French lost more than 200,000 men along the Aisne. The French troops by now were completely disgusted with their generals. One frustrated regiment marched to the front bleating like sheep being led to the slaughter. On April 29, 1917, mutiny broke out in another French regiment. More widespread mutiny followed. Thousands of troops rioted, threw down their rifles, and refused to obey their officers' orders. Many French soldiers deserted their stations. Great stretches of front were left undefended.

General Pétain quickly stepped in to restore order out of chaos. More than 100,000 soldiers were court-martialed. Military courts found 23,000 guilty. Of those, 432 were sentenced to death and 55 were executed. The French soldiers returned to the trenches. But three years of brutal war had broken their spirit completely.

Russia Bows Out

The year 1917 shook the heart of Russia as well. Throughout the previous year, the Russians suffered severe losses along the Eastern Front. On June 4, 1916, General Aleksei Brusilov's Russian Army simply attacked at twenty different points, hoping to crack the enemy battle line. The Russians took 250,000 prisoners on the Austro-Hungarian front. But the Germans struck back, forcing Brusilov to retreat. In the end, the Russians suffered more than 1 million casualties in the campaign. To fill its empty ranks, the Russian Army dragged peasants off their farms. Without farmers to grow crops, Russian marketplaces became bare of food. The masses turned against the czar, blaming him for their defeats. Hungry Russian soldiers at the front angrily chanted "Bread and Peace." Russian revolutionaries, known as Bolsheviks, added a demand for "Land."

Finally, food riots broke out in Petrograd (present-day St. Petersburg), which was then the Russian capital. On March 11, 1917, police using machine guns killed more than two hundred demonstrators in street fighting. The local army garrison mutinied after being ordered to support the police. Instead, the soldiers joined in the looting of stores and warehouses. Russian government official Mikhail Rodzianko anxiously wired the czar: "Anarchy reigns in the capital."

At his military headquarters, Czar Nicholas II seemed powerless. As his empire crumbled around him, the czar's generals advised him to abdicate. On March 26, Czar Nicholas II signed a paper giving up his throne. The Romanov dynasty had ended. Workers and soldiers swiftly grabbed control of the government in Petrograd.

Calling themselves a council, or "soviet," they set up a provisional government of liberal politicians. Alexander Kerensky took the lead in the new government's affairs. At first, there was no talk of quitting the war.

One man thought differently, however. This was Vladimir Lenin, the Bolshevik leader who was in exile in Zurich, Switzerland. Lenin (his real name was Vladimir Ilich Ulyanov) was not interested in defeating the Germans. He wanted to establish a Socialist government in Russia. Lenin determined to return to Russia at once to take advantage of the turmoil. Ludendorff, eager to weaken Russia, let Lenin pass through Germany on a special train. Lenin arrived in Petrograd on April 16, 1917. He was showered with bouquets of roses by waiting comrades. Lenin at once denounced the provisional government and began to preach a new revolution. "What do you get from war?" he asked street crowds. "Only wounds, starvation, and death."

On the Eastern Front, the Russian Army was falling apart. In July 1917, the Russian soldiers lurched against the German lines one last time. After that, disheartened Russian soldiers simply began to quit fighting. Thousands filled the roads heading east, toward home. In October, rebellious regiments stationed in Petrograd announced: "We no longer recognize the Provisional Government." Kerensky left Petrograd on November 7, 1917, never to return.

A chaotic scene on the main street in Petrograd, Russia, during the Russian Revolution in May 1917. Food riots broke out in the capital city, and police killed many civilians.

That evening, Bolshevik volunteers called "Red Guards" captured the Winter Palace and arrested the remaining members of the provisional government. Only six Red Guards died in the Bolshevik Revolution that brought Lenin to power in Russia.

Bolshevik leader Leon Trotsky met with German officials at Brest Litovsk in February 1918. Trotsky proposed a military truce between Russia and Germany. With no enemy in front of them, however, the Germans instead marched onward, taking hundreds of miles of Russian territory. At last, Russia agreed to sign a peace treaty on any terms the Germans offered. On March 3, 1918, Russia signed the treaty of Brest Litovsk, in which they gave up Lithuania, Latvia, Estonia, Poland, and the Ukraine. "This is a peace that Russia, grinding her teeth, is forced to accept," Trotsky bitterly declared.[8] With the fighting now ended on the Eastern Front, Germany turned its full attention to the West.

3

THE YANKS ARE COMING

O-VER THERE, O-VER THERE, SEND THE WORD, SEND THE WORD O-VER THERE,
THAT THE YANKS ARE COM-ING, THE YANKS ARE COM-ING,
THE DRUMS RUM-TUM-MING EV'-RY WHERE.

SO PRE-PARE, SAY A PRAY'R, SEND THE WORD, SEND THE WORD TO BE-WARE,
WE'LL BE O-VER, WE'RE COMING O-VER,
AND WE WON'T COME BACK 'TIL IT'S O-VER O-VER THERE!

—Chorus from the 1917 American song "Over There" by George M. Cohan

"He Kept Us Out of War," was the campaign slogan that helped President Woodrow Wilson win reelection in 1916. In fact, America prospered because of the war. American farmers sold wheat, cotton, and other crops to both the Allies and the Central Powers. American factories sold guns, ammunition, and other war supplies to both sides. Peace-loving Americans sang a popular song entitled, "I Didn't Raise My Boy to Be a Soldier." The United States remained neutral in feelings until the Germans began sinking merchant ships.

Safe for Democracy

When a German torpedo sank the passenger liner *Lusitania* on May 7, 1915, Americans in great numbers began to favor the Allies.

4

RENDEZVOUS
WITH DEATH

I HAVE A RENDEZVOUS WITH DEATH
AT SOME DISPUTED BARRICADE,
WHEN SPRING COMES BACK WITH RUSTLING SHADE
AND APPLE BLOSSOMS FILL THE AIR . . .

—From the poem "I Have a Rendezvous With Death"
by American poet and soldier Alan Seeger

"He Kept Us Out of War," was the campaign slogan that helped President Woodrow Wilson win reelection in 1916. In fact, America prospered because of the war. American farmers sold wheat, cotton, and other crops to both the Allies and the Central Powers. American factories sold guns, ammunition, and other war supplies to both sides. Peace-loving Americans sang a popular song entitled, "I Didn't Raise My Boy to Be a Soldier." The United States remained neutral in feelings until the Germans began sinking merchant ships.

Safe for Democracy

When a German torpedo sank the passenger liner *Lusitania* on May 7, 1915, Americans in great numbers began to favor the Allies.

Some fiery young Americans joined the French Foreign Legion. Others slipped over the border into Canada and to fight with the British royal forces. About two hundred adventurous Americans flew with the French air force. The American Red Cross, the Norton-Harjes, and the American Field Service provided volunteer ambulance drivers to aid wounded British and French forces.

• • • • • • • • • • • • • • • • • •

All shipping in the Atlantic war zone would be sunk on sight, Germany said.

• • • • • • • • • • • • • • • • • •

After promising to stop its unrestricted submarine warfare, Germany began it again in January 1917. All shipping in the Atlantic war zone would be sunk on sight, Germany said. U.S. president Wilson swiftly reacted, breaking diplomatic relations with Germany. Later, he released to the public the contents of a German message that had recently been intercepted by the British Secret Service. The "Zimmerman telegram" revealed a plan by the German secretary of state to draw Mexico into war against the United States.

In March 1917, German submarines sank three American ships. War fever heightened throughout the United States. Former president Theodore Roosevelt thundered, "There is no question about going to war. Germany is already at war with us." People marched in preparedness parades in cities across the country, carrying banners that read: "Kill the Kaiser!" "On to Berlin!" and "Let's Get the Hun!"

Finally, President Wilson called for a special session of Congress. On the warm, rainy night of April 2, 1917, spectators jammed the galleries of the U.S. House of Representatives. Many congressmen wore small American flags in their lapels. Wilson stepped before them and declared: "The present German submarine warfare against commerce is a war against mankind. It is a war against all nations. . . . We are accepting this challenge. . . . We are glad . . . to fight . . . for the ultimate peace of the world. . . . The world must be made safe for democracy."[1]

Wilson asked Congress to declare war on Germany. In the midnight hours of April 5 to 6, the Senate voted 82 to 6 to declare war. In the House of Representatives, the vote for war was 373 to 50. Soon, the president officially announced: "I, Woodrow Wilson, President of the United States of America, do hereby proclaim to all whom it may concern that a state of war exists between the United States and the Imperial German Government."

I WANT YOU!

"We came into this war without an army," General John J. Pershing declared, "so now we must build an entire organization." The United States possessed a powerful navy of three hundred ships in 1917, but almost no army. In a nation of 70 million people, there were only about 200,000 regular soldiers and National Guardsmen.

The government decided that the American Expeditionary Force would be composed mainly of draftees. The first Selective Service Act passed in Congress on May 17, 1917. Under the act, all men ages twenty-one to thirty were required to register for a draft. Later, the age limits were extended from eighteen to forty-five. Altogether, more than 24 million men registered. Of these, 4.8 million were drafted or volunteered. The selection process began on July 20 when Secretary of War Newton D. Baker put on a blindfold. He reached into a large glass jar and pulled out the number 258. The man holding that number in each local draft board area was called up.

Many Americans were eager to serve. "To the youth of America," recalled Lieutenant George C. Kenney, "World War I was the Great Adventure. Very few of them had ever been outside the United States, but now, after Uncle

During the second draft, Secretary of War Newton D. Baker picks out a number from a glass jar while blindfolded in June 1918. The first draft began on July 20, 1917, when Baker selected the number 258.

Sam trained them . . . they would have an opportunity to visit France."[2]

All these new soldiers had to be housed and trained. In the summer of 1917, two hundred thousand carpenters, plumbers, and electricians rushed to build thirty-two new military camps for the recruits being gathered.

Each of the newly organized military units had its own special flavor. Because the New

Yorkers in the new 77th Division included so many sons of immigrants, it came to be called the "Liberty Division" after the Statue of Liberty in New York Harbor. The Irish Americans who filled the New York City 69th National Guard Regiment proudly called themselves the "Fighting 69th." National Guardsmen from the New England states filled the 26th Division. They called themselves the "Yankee Division." The 42nd Division was made up of men from twenty-six different states and the District of Columbia. One of its officers, Douglas MacArthur, suggested it be named the "Rainbow Division."

A young army recruit practices bayonet fighting with his drilling instructor at Camp Dick, Texas. Soldiers drilled for many hours during basic training before going to Europe.

"It will stretch across the nation like a rainbow," he proudly noted.

The typical recruit was between the ages of twenty-one and twenty-three and a bachelor. He stood 5 feet, 7 inches tall and weighed around 141 pounds. His uniform was made of drab olive wool. It consisted of a high-collared blouse, trousers, a broad-brimmed peaked campaign hat, and leggings that wrapped from ankle to shin. For the recruits, drill, fieldwork, inspection, and reviews filled six days every week. Until there were enough rifles to go around, many men drilled with broomsticks. At Fort Sheridan, Illinois, recruit Frederick T. Edwards wrote to his sister: "We get up at 5:15; and from then, until ten o'clock at night every hour is taken." Recruit Samuel M. Wilson later declared, "We drilled and fought dummies with bayonets until we couldn't see straight."

"You can bet we drilled those men hard," recalled Lieutenant Mark Clark. "I drilled them, hiked them, ran them; believe me, every minute for months we were on them. I didn't want to lose any lives because they weren't tough enough."

War Work

"It is not an army that we must shape and train for war. It is a nation," declared Woodrow Wilson. In 1917, the U.S. Army possessed only 285,000 Springfield rifles, about 400 pieces of field artillery, and fewer than 1,500 machine guns. The aviation section of the Army Signal Corps possessed fifty-five out-of-date biplanes.

Bond-drive posters crying "Buy Liberty Bonds!" were everywhere, persuading citizens to contribute to the war effort. The purchases of Liberty Bonds, Victory Bonds, war savings certificates, and thrift stamps raised $23 billion. Film stars such as Douglas Fairbanks, Sr., Mary Pickford, and Charlie Chaplin tried to outdo each other in selling war bonds at public rallies. Girl Scouts collected peach stones to be burned and made into charcoal for gas-mask filters. Boy Scouts collected scrap metal. The Red Cross, the YMCA, the Salvation Army, and other volunteer organizations swarmed about training camps, handing out refreshments and putting on church services, shows, and dances.

In a great propaganda campaign, newspapers, books, posters, and films all promoted the war effort and attacked "Kaiser Bill" and the Germans. Americans turned their backs on everything German. Hamburgers were given a new name—"Liberty Steak." Sauerkraut became "Liberty Cabbage," and dachshunds were renamed "Liberty Pups." American songwriters composed patriotic tunes, such as "K-K-K-Katy," "Goodbye Broadway—Hello France," and "We're All Going Calling on the Kaiser." British war songs such as "Tipperary," "Pack Up Your Troubles,"

This is a recruitment poster for the U.S. Army used during World War I.

and "Mademoiselle from Armentieres," also became very popular in the United States.

Americans prepared to send tons of food, ammunition, and supplies to Europe. To "Hooverize" meant to save food for the people in war-torn Europe. Encouraging wheatless and meatless days was a part of the campaign waged by U.S. food administrator Herbert Hoover. As early as 1914, Hoover had organized food programs to feed the starving people of Belgium.

President Wilson named Secretary of the Treasury William G. McAdoo to take control of America's railroads and keep them running smoothly during the war. As chairman of the War Industries Board, Bernard Baruch took charge of many American industries. Baruch, a wealthy Wall Street speculator, had a mind like a computer. Wilson called him "Dr. Facts." "The means of controlling the war effort," Baruch later stated, was knowing "who gets what and when."

Howard E. Coffin, a vice president of the Hudson Motor Car Company, declared, "Twentieth-century warfare demands that the blood of the soldier must be mingled with from three to five parts of the sweat of the man in the factories, mills, mines, and fields of the nation in arms."[3] Thousands of African Americans and American women found work opportunities they had never had before. The wartime production of U.S. factories was astonishing. They produced

American women work in a factory wrapping rockets during World War I. The war provided many women with new employment opportunities.

9.5 million army overcoats, 34 million pairs of shoes, 3.1 million rifles, 5.4 million gas masks, 22 million blankets, tons of machinery and equipment, and great numbers of trucks and locomotives.

Black Jack Pershing

On May 7, 1917, fifty-six-year-old Brigadier General John J. Pershing noted in his diary: "Was informed by the Secretary of War that I was to command the American troops in France; and that I should be prepared to leave for France as soon as possible."

Pershing seemed the perfect choice for the job. A year earlier, on March 9, 1916, Mexican revolutionary leader Pancho Villa had led a raid into Columbus, New Mexico, killing fifteen Americans and wounding thirteen others. President Wilson swiftly called out units of the U.S. National Guard. A 12,000-man U.S. Army punitive expedition commanded by Pershing soon marched into Mexico to track down Villa. Though Pershing's force failed to catch Villa, the troops got in one year of hard field service and gained a lasting nickname. As they hiked over the adobe soil of Mexico, the men often became covered with powdery dust. As a result they were called "adobes," which later became "doughboys."

• • • • • • • • • • • • • • • • • • • •

As a result they were called "adobes," which later became "doughboys."

• • • • • • • • • • • • • • • • • • •

Born in Laclede, Missouri, and a graduate of the U.S. Military Academy at West Point, class of 1886, Pershing already had earned respect as a tough veteran soldier. In the American West, he served with African-American regiments, which later suggested his nickname of "Black Jack." In the Spanish-American War of 1898, Lieutenant Pershing charged up San Juan Hill in Cuba with the Tenth Cavalry Regiment. In the Philippines in 1902 to 1903, Captain Pershing led U.S. forces against the native Moros.

Called to Washington, D.C., in 1917, Pershing was promoted to the command of the American Expeditionary Force (AEF). On May 29, 1917, the British liner *Baltic* sailed from New York with Pershing and 187 staff officers, enlisted men, and clerks on board. After first stopping in England, it continued on to Boulogne, France, reaching there on June 13. American newspaperman Floyd Gibbons witnessed Pershing's arrival:

> The crowds overflowed the sidewalks. . . . From the . . . balconies and windows overlooking the route, women and children tossed down showers of flowers and bits of colored cloth. . . . Old gray-haired fathers of French fighting men bared their heads and with tears steaming down their cheeks shouted greetings to the tall, thin, gray-mustached American commander who was leading new armies to the support of their sons.[4]

To the Front

"We want men, men, men," French marshal Joffre plainly told the United States. With basic training hardly completed, American soldiers traveled from all across the United States to New York, because most of the soldiers left the country from there. All along the railway tracks, people waved flags and cheered as troop trains roared past. In New York Harbor, soldiers with full packs moved steadily up ship gangplanks.

American soldiers wave good-bye on board a ship going to France to join the Allies in Europe.

Private William H. Houghton's ship was the USS *George Washington*. He never forgot leaving the harbor. "I stood on deck watching America disappear from view," he later remarked. "It was the first time in my life I'd been out of sight of land."

Sergeant George Krahnert remembered his crossing with the First Division in June 1917: "I was on the San Jacinto. . . . We were packed like sardines. You couldn't have fit . . . more troops on her if you used a shoehorn." Aboard the British ship *Justian*, Corporal Michael Shallin recalled, "It was hardly a joy ride. It seems all they kept feeding us was rabbit stew, and I swear, it still had the fur on it." The largest troop ship was the *Leviathan*. In ten trips, the *Leviathan* carried 96,804 soldiers to Europe.

German submarines posed a very real danger during these Atlantic crossings. In March and April 1917, more than a million tons of British and neutral shipping had been sunk. Britain's admiral Sir John Jellicoe exclaimed, "It is impossible for us to go on with the war if losses like this continue."[5]

But the Allies soon learned how to combat the U-boat menace. They ran merchant ships across the Atlantic in convoys. In these convoys, dozens of ships sailing together were protected by circling navy destroyers. The destroyers dropped newly developed depth charges (three-hundred-pound cans of the explosive TNT) upon the submerged submarines they chased. By September 17, 1917, shipping losses to enemy submarines had fallen to one percent.

Pershing and his staff developed the Services of Supply (SOS) to feed and supply the "Yanks" arriving in France. In France, the SOS built its own dock facilities at various French ports, laid a thousand miles of railroad, put up refrigeration and baking plants, and even built candy factories.

America's first troops arrived at Saint-Nazaire, France, at the end of June 1917. These 14,000 men included the army's First Division and a regiment of Marines. "They are sturdy rookies," commented Pershing. "We shall make great soldiers of them." One battalion from the First Division paraded through Paris on July 4, 1917. "Vive les Americains!" shouted the French as bands blared military tunes. Excited men and women hugged and kissed these first American soldiers. Pershing remembered seeing "many women forcing their way into the ranks and swinging along arm in arm with the men. With wreaths about their necks and bouquets in their hats and rifles, the column looked like a moving flower garden."

The ceremonies that Fourth of July included a visit to Picpus Cemetery in Paris, the burial place of the Marquis de Lafayette. In 1777, during the American Revolution, the young Lafayette had sailed to

General John "Black Jack" Pershing at his headquarters in Chaumont, France, on October 19, 1918.

America at his own expense and had served bravely in the Continental army as a major general under General George Washington. Americans felt they owed a debt to such a hero. Standing before his tomb, Lieutenant Colonel Charles E. Stanton of the United States solemnly proclaimed, "Lafayette, we are here!"

In September 1917, Pershing established his headquarters at Chaumont near the Marne River. There, he set about building America's army in Europe. American staff officer Colonel Charles Dawes declared, "Pershing is the man for this great emergency. He has an immense faculty for disposing of things. He is not only a great soldier, but he has great common sense and tremendous energy."

"We are all working very hard here in France," wrote Pershing, "trying to get things in shape for the large part we are to play in this great war drama." The 26th Division arrived in September. A brigade of Marines and several army units also arrived that month, and they were formed into the new Second Division. In October 1917, soldiers of the 42nd Division stepped ashore in France. The Americans were arriving just as fast as they could. Once they landed at French ports, the Yanks piled onto "40 and 8s," French railroad cars designed to hold forty soldiers and eight horses.

On their way to the front, some lucky soldiers had time to visit Paris. Roaming "Gay Par-ee,"

American soldiers visited the Eiffel Tower and the Arc de Triomphe. They dined at Maxim's and Ciro's restaurants and cheered the "can-can" girls at the Folies Bergeré. Exclaimed Lieutenant George C. Kenney, "We intended having some fun in Paris before we went to war."

Behind the front lines, the American troops first trained under the French. The First Division built a large, realistic trench complex near Gondrecourt. Veteran French troops of the 47th Chasseur Alpine Division (called the Blue Devils) taught the inexperienced American soldiers how to use weapons, such as the French Chauchat

American soldiers in the 329th Infantry Regiment, 83rd Division, practice hand grenade drills at Le Mans, France, in October 1918. Veteran French troops trained the first American soldiers arriving in Europe before sending them to the front lines.

automatic rifle and the British Hotchkiss machine gun. The Yanks learned bayonet and grenade techniques. The French instructors also showed them how to use flamethrowers and how to defend against gas attacks.

At last, the time arrived for the American divisions to fill places in the Allied battle line. Marine corporal J. E. Rendinell never forgot traveling by truck toward the front: "The people in these small villages ran out [and] yelled 'The Americans are coming.' . . . Children were yelling 'Vive l'Amerique.'"

First Blood

After training through the summer, the U.S. First Division was the first American unit to reach the front lines. On October 23, 1917, a battery from the Sixth Field Artillery of the First Division was stationed temporarily in the Toul section of the battle line. It fired the first U.S. Army cannon of the war. Sergeant Alex Arch pulled the lanyard and sent the shell soaring.

On November 2, near midnight, a little more than a week later, the Germans staged a trench raid in the same section. German mortar shells smashed into the American line, and machine guns spit streams of bullets toward the Yankee trenches. In the confusion, a German assault company cut through the barbed wire without being discovered. The raiders slipped into an American trench, did their bloody work, and got away, all within ten minutes. "The enemy was very good in hand-to-hand fighting," reported the German lieutenant who led the raid. The Germans left behind three of their own dead and took eleven prisoners. They also killed three Americans. Corporal James B. Gresham, Private Thomas F. Enright, and Private Merle D. Hay were the first Americans killed in the war.

• •

Corporal James B. Gresham, Private Thomas F. Enright, and Private Merle D. Hay were the first Americans killed in the war.

• •

On the night of April 20–21, 1918, the Germans staged a surprise raid on a quiet training area in the Lorraine region. At the village of Seicheprey, about three thousand German shock troops fell on three companies of about six hundred men of the American 26th Division. The Yanks fought hard. Major George Rau of the 102nd Infantry Battalion ordered his cooks, truck drivers, and other arriving reinforcements into the fight. In the end, the Germans inflicted some 650 casualties, including 81 killed. The Germans used their small victory at Seicheprey as propaganda. Soon afterward, German airplanes dropped photos of captured Americans along the Allied lines. "Are these the

men who are going to save the war for you?"
the captions taunted.[6]

The Americans staged their first attack on
the enemy on May 28, 1918. Advancing under
a heavy artillery barrage, about four thousand
Yanks of the First Division commanded by Major
General Robert Lee Bullard stormed the village
of Cantigny. Before the Germans could prepare
their machine guns, the Americans rushed into
the streets. They bayoneted Germans in their
trenches and hurled grenades. Flamethrowers
sprayed liquid fire into enemy dugouts. American
lieutenant Clarence R. Huebner remembered
seeing one burned German. He "ran ten to
fifteen yards then fell over singed to death."

The Yanks captured the town and fought off
German counterattacks over the next three days.
Altogether, the Germans suffered some 1,600
killed, wounded, and captured in the bloody
struggle at Cantigny. The Americans suffered
1,067 casualties. But they had proved that they
could fight.

RENDEZVOUS WITH DEATH

I HAVE A RENDEZVOUS WITH DEATH
AT SOME DISPUTED BARRICADE,
WHEN SPRING COMES BACK WITH RUSTLING SHADE
AND APPLE BLOSSOMS FILL THE AIR . . .

—From the poem "I Have a Rendezvous With Death"
by American poet and soldier Alan Seeger

In the spring of 1918, American troops thrust themselves full force into the nightmare that was World War I. In the following months, battles at Belleau Wood, the Marne, and Saint-Mihiel would write bloody pages in our nation's history book.

Life in the Trenches

American troops began reaching the Western Front in great numbers during the first months of 1918. In the Picardy sector, the American First Division began its life in the trenches. The deep trenches were wickered and sand-bagged, and long crosscuts were added to prevent damage by shell bursts and mortar fire. Most trenches were deeper than a man's height and about a yard wide. The walls were reinforced by a kind of fence work made by interlacing wooden sticks. "Duck boards," a kind of wooden sidewalk, stretched along the bottom to make walking easier.

The soldiers rose at dawn and breakfasted on hardtack crackers, bacon, and coffee. Rolling kitchens behind the lines prepared hot food and sent it up. Cooks made mush from cornmeal and fried tinned salmon, which they called "goldfish." The soldiers called beef stew "slumgullion" and the stringy corned beef they ate "monkey meat."

During the winter months of 1918, the Western Front experienced no great battles. Poisonous gas clouds sometimes drifted over.

Life in the trenches was extremely dangerous and difficult. It could also get very boring between battles. In this photo, American soldiers stand ready in their trenches in France.

The night skies over the shell-cratered middle ground often glowed with artillery fireworks. Soldiers were killed or wounded by snipers while on guard duty. At night, patrols crawled out into No-Man's-Land to listen for any enemy activity. Sergeant Merritt D. Cutler of the 27th Division remembered, "it was frightening to realize that you were only fifty to a hundred yards away from some men whose main aim was to kill you."

Sergeant Earl Goldsmith of the 32nd Division found one way to fight off boredom. "Most of the time our biggest excitement was rat shooting," he recalled. "God, were they big! Some looked like small dogs." Private Philip H. Hammerslough remembered the filth of the trenches:

> Each trench section had dugouts with bunks. You'd take your turn standing in the trenches, then go back into the dugouts. The bunks were all full of cooties. During . . . six weeks I never took a bath. . . . When we left that area, . . . they took us to this medical center where they . . . took all our cruddy clothing and burned it. Did it stink!

Most soldiers found the gas mask with its nose clamp, mouthpiece, and clouding goggles very uncomfortable but necessary. Medical officer Bernard J. Gallagher, an American fighting with the British, survived one gas attack. "I must have inhaled a lot of gas," he later explained. "I suddenly found myself on my back, gasping for breath, unable to get any air into my lungs, and deathly sick at my stomach. I was able to get my gas mask on, and a few whiffs of air through that put me right again."[1] Troops exposed to exploding gas shells were evacuated in long lines. Like blind men, they walked with their hands upon the shoulders of the man ahead, coughing and vomiting, their eyes sticking shut. The most frightening gas was mustard gas. No mask was proof against it. It burned through clothing and flesh, raising painful blisters, destroying vision, and choking out life.

• • • • • • • • • • • • • • • • • • • •

"Some of them cursed and raved . . . some shook violently . . . some trembled . . . while others simply stood speechless."

• • • • • • • • • • • • • • • • • • • •

The constant pounding of artillery shells caused another major battlefield problem: shell shock. Medical officer Major William E. Boyce described a few shell-shock victims he saw: "Some of them cursed and raved . . . some shook violently . . . some trembled . . . while others simply stood speechless." Sergeant Merritt D. Cutler later explained, "Real shell shock was the actual scrambling of a man's brain by concussion. If you've ever seen a man actually lose his wits through shelling, you'd never forget it. The poor guys became jibbering idiots."

Living in the trenches between January and April 1918 molded the Americans into hardened troops. "It was this period that made us tough," declared Marine Sergeant Gerald C. Thomas. "We got tough, we stayed tough."

The Kaiser's Gamble

"The German High Command . . . knew the Americans were landing in force now in France," U.S. Marine Lieutenant Samuel Meek remembered, "and they had to break the Allies before the United States could throw a million or more fresh troops at them." German general Erich Ludendorff rushed fifty-two divisions from the now quiet Eastern Front to take part in a great offensive. On the Western Front, the German army swelled to 3.5 million men.

"Michael," the code name for the German offensive, opened on the foggy morning of March 21, 1918. German troops struck at the point where the three-hundred-mile French line joined the one-hundred-mile British line. Ludendorff planned to split the Allied forces, capture the Channel ports, and outflank Paris from the north. The British defenders found themselves outnumbered four to one. The German divisions smashed a hole in the line fifty miles wide and up to forty miles deep. In four days, they crushed the British Fifth Army. On March 23, the people of Paris were stunned when the first shells from three enormous

German guns called the "Paris Guns" crashed in the streets of the city. Every twenty minutes, the guns fired from seventy-one miles away.

At a meeting on March 26, French marshal Ferdinand Foch asked the French and British war leaders present, "Why aren't you fighting? I would fight without break. I would fight in front of Amiens . . . I would fight all the time." To meet the German threat, Foch was appointed commander in chief of all the Allied forces in France. "We are ready and anxious for a chance to do our part in the fight," General John Pershing had already told Foch. "Infantry, artillery, aviation, all that we have is yours; use it as you wish."[2] There were more than 500,000 American troops in France by then. Pershing agreed that American divisions would take important places in the battle line.

• • • • • • • • • • • • • • • • • •

"Infantry, artillery, aviation, all that we have is yours; use it as you wish."

• • • • • • • • • • • • • • • • • •

By the end of May 1918, the Germans were heading for the Marne River. Ludendorff hurled thirty divisions against the French, captured the city of Soissons, and pushed south toward the riverside village of Chateau-Thierry. The advancing Germans seized 650 artillery pieces, 2,000 machine guns, and 60,000 French prisoners.

The enemy was now within fifty miles of Paris and heading toward open, flat country. Only exhausted French troops stood between them and the capital. Marshal Foch ordered the U.S. Second and Third Divisions up to the Marne to plug the opening gap.

The Seventh Machine Gun Battalion of the American Third Division rushed into action. After a 110-mile journey that took twenty-two hours in overloaded trucks, it arrived at Chateau-Thierry on the afternoon of May 31. Lieutenant John T. Bissell and fourteen enlisted men hurried across an important wagon bridge carrying two Hotchkiss heavy machine guns. Bravely, they held off one advancing column of Germans. Additional arriving Third Division troops took positions on other Marne bridges at Chateau-Thierry. These machine gunners, reinforced by French Moroccans and the American Second Division, stalled the Germans on the other side of the Marne River and blocked the way to Paris.

Belleau Wood

A small forest less than a mile wide and two miles deep, called the Belleau Wood, stood just west of Chateau-Thierry. Veteran German troops advanced among the trees. They concealed machine-gun nests behind rocks and in the thick underbrush. Mortars and artillery were set up to fire upon the open fields leading to the woods.

General Pershing ordered the Second Division to capture the important position. The Second Division, 25,000 men strong, contained a brigade of regular Marines and a brigade of volunteer army troops. Nearing the Belleau Wood, some Marines met French soldiers retreating to the rear. The Frenchmen called for the Americans to turn back. "Retreat, hell," answered Marine colonel Wendell C. Neville, "we just got here!"

The Germans were very surprised when the Americans replaced the exhausted French. Marine lieutenant Lemuel Shepherd later remembered, "The Germans [were] attacking, and we're knocking the hell out of them with rifle fire, which was something they obviously didn't expect. . . . I guess the Germans didn't realize they were coming against Americans. We could actually hear them yelling about it." From June 1 to June 5, 1918, these Yanks kept the Germans from advancing beyond the wood. Marine corporal J. E. Rendinell recalled one German attack: "How we raked the German ranks. We all took careful aim before every shot. My gun got so hot I could not touch it."

On June 6, Marine brigadier general James Harbord ordered his brigade to rush Belleau Wood. The Marines crawled from rock to rock under withering machine-gun fire. "I saw one sergeant literally climb up on the top of a machine-gun nest, driving down into the

In this painting, American soldiers of the 30th and 38th regiments fight off a heavy German attack during a battle at the Marne River. This brave group of soldiers became known as "The Rock of the Marne" for holding off thousands of German troops.

by capturing machine-gun nests at the point of the bayonet.

By nightfall of July 19, the second day of the battle, the Americans had advanced more than five miles into the German lines, capturing the vital highway from Soissons to Chateau-Thierry. But the cost was very high. The First Division had suffered some four thousand casualties. The Second Division lost more than seven thousand men killed, wounded, or missing. "Battalions looked like companies, companies like squads," grimly remembered Brigadier General Beaumont B. Buck.

To push the Germans completely back across the Marne, the 42nd and 4th divisions next attacked in the region of the Ourcq River at the end of July. The Fourth Division was the least trained of the troops. Some of the soldiers barely knew how to put the bullet clips into their rifles. But they advanced and held. By August 26, the 28th, 32nd, and 3rd divisions also had joined in the successful Allied push toward the Marne. Meanwhile, on August 8, a British-led army had attacked farther north, near the Belgium border. Within a few days, the Germans had been thrown back beyond positions that they had held since 1914. General Ludendorff admitted unhappily, "8 August was the black day of the German Army in the history of this war." From that day forward, the Germans remained on the defensive.

Saint-Mihiel

"The time may come when the American Army will have to stand the brunt of this war," General Pershing declared. "It would be a grave mistake to give up the idea of building an American Army in all its details as rapidly as possible." By August 1918, there were 1.2 million Yanks in France. More were arriving at the rate of ten thousand a day. Until now, the U.S. divisions had fought scattered among the French and British armies. But Pershing's dream was to command a

united and independent American army. The
French and British finally agreed.

On August 30, 1918, Pershing proudly took
command of the U.S. First Army's 555,000 men
along a forty-mile sector that bounded the town
of Saint-Mihiel. Within days, he sent an order to
his generals: "The First Army will reduce the St.
Mihiel salient." Where the German battle line
bulged around the town of Saint-Mihiel,

• • • • • • • • • • • • • • • • • • •
*"At exactly 1 A.M. the artillery cut
loose. It seemed as if all the artillery in
France had suddenly opened up."*
• • • • • • • • • • • • • • • • • • •

an American attack was to force them back and
straighten out the line. Staff officer Colonel
George C. Marshall designed much of the plan.

From flank to flank, 665,000 soldiers,
including 110,000 Frenchmen, assembled for the
battle. Moving secretly at night, on muddy roads,
they marched in long columns to reach their
assigned positions. Horses struggled to pull
three thousand artillery pieces and hundreds of
ammunition wagons through the mire.

On September 12, 1918, the Allied offensive
began. Lieutenant Phelps Harding of the 77th
Division later exclaimed: "At exactly 1 A.M. the
artillery cut loose. It seemed as if all the artillery
in France had suddenly opened up. The sky was

General Pershing took command of the first independent American army in August 1918. His army's first mission was to take back the Saint-Mihiel region in France. In this photo, American soldiers take a rest in a ruined French town near Saint-Mihiel.

red with big flashes . . . and the explosions of the heavier shells made the ground tremble."

"I'd been out on a patrol the night before," recalled Sergeant Russell Adams of the 26th Division. "I'd seen all this barbed wire the Germans had set up. I was scared to death when I thought what it would be like to charge through it. Then we had that barrage. . . . Why, all that barbed wire just disappeared—t'wasn't nothing to it."[5]

At 5:00 A.M., the Allied divisions advanced through a morning fog. By chance, the Germans were in the process of drawing back from Saint-Mihiel when the Americans attacked. They were unprepared for a hard battle. The American troops moved steadily across the broken ground.

The first waves overran the enemy front-line trenches, capturing Germans in swarms. Sergeant Harry J. Adams of the 89th Division called into one dugout for the enemy to surrender. He was surprised when three hundred Germans poured out with their hands up.

By nightfall of the first day, most of the U.S. First Army had already reached the objectives assigned for the second day. The offensive liberated two hundred square miles of French territory. "At the cost of only 7,000 casualties, mostly light, we had taken 16,000 prisoners and 443 guns," happily declared General Pershing. On September 14, President Wilson telegraphed his congratulations. "The boys have done what we expected of them and done it in the way we most admire. We are deeply proud of them and their Chief." The Battle of Saint-Mihiel had been a great American success.

Knights of the Sky

"The only interest and romance in this war was in the air," insisted American brigadier general Billy Mitchell. Nothing caught the imagination of the public as much as the thrill of airplane battles in the sky over France. High above the muddy trenches, German and Allied pilots soared at one hundred miles an hour, dueling with each other in "dogfights." These warriors of the air received much newspaper attention and became celebrities.

American ace pilots of the Lafayette Escadrille *photographed in France during World War I.*

In the early days of the war, pilots served mostly as aerial observers reporting troop movements and artillery positions. Before long, they mounted machine guns on their planes and began firing at one another. Some planes carried two men, but the most famous pilots flew single-seater pursuit planes. The British developed sixty-seven different types of observation, pursuit, and day-and-night bombing aircraft. The French manufactured sixty-four different kinds. These new aircraft included the famous British Bristol and the French Spad.

When an aviator shot down five or more enemy planes he became an "ace." Canadian ace William Bishop scored seventy "kills." French ace Captain René Fonck was credited with seventy-five kills by war's end. On May 8, 1918,

Fonck brought down six airplanes while firing only fifty-six shots. The Germans had their air heroes, too. Germany's Baron Manfred von Richthofen commanded a squadron of brightly colored planes known as "the Flying Circus." His own plane was painted red, and he was called "the Red Baron." Richthofen shot down eighty planes before being shot down himself in September 1918. When General Ludendorff learned of his death, he mourned, "He was worth as much to us as three divisions."

At the beginning of the war, American flyers enlisted in the French Air Service. Developing into first-rate pilots, they won fame as the *Lafayette Escadrille* (Lafayette Squadron). When the United States declared war, some thirty-eight of these veteran pilots transferred to the Aviation Section of the U.S. Army Signal Corps.

At their training center at Issoudun, France, new American pilots learned to fly the Nieuport, a French pursuit plane. The first American pursuit squadron was the 94th Squadron. On the sides of their planes, they painted pictures of Uncle Sam's hat with a ring around it. They called themselves "The Hat in the Ring Squadron." Major Raoul Lufbery, famed American veteran of the *Lafayette Escadrille*, with seventeen kills, was the training officer of the 94th. In May 1918, Lufbery's plane burst into flames while he was under attack. He jumped from the burning plane and fell to his death.

In this illustration, an American ace of the 94th Squadron maneuvers in a dogfight against German planes on October 22, 1918, in France.

On April 14, 1918, Lieutenant Douglas Campbell scored the first kill by a pilot in the American service. In July, Campbell became the first American ace, with his fifth kill above the ruined bridges of Chateau-Thierry. "Nobody had any plans for tomorrow," Campbell later declared of his dangerous flying career.

The best American ace, Captain Eddie Rickenbacker, shot down twenty-six German planes in the aerial dogfights. Rickenbacker, a professional race car driver before the war, started his army career as a chauffeur for General Pershing. On April 29, 1918, Rickenbacker attacked his first German plane, a Pfalz. The German pilot, Rickenbacker remembered,

was running like a scared rabbit. I was gaining
upon him every instant and I had my sights trained
dead upon his seat. . . . At 150 yards I pressed my
triggers. The tracer bullets cut a streak of living fire
into the rear of the Pfalz tail. . . . The Pfalz circled
a little to the south and the next minute crashed
onto the ground. . . . I had brought down my first
enemy aeroplane.[6]

Lieutenant Frank Luke of the 95th "Kicking
Mule" Squadron loved shooting down enemy
observation balloons. If enemy planes showed
up, he also battled them with reckless glee.
Luke once recorded five kills (two observation
balloons and three planes) in just five minutes.
Finally, shot down behind German lines on
September 29, 1918, Luke landed safely on the
ground. Refusing to surrender to enemy soldiers,
he tried to shoot his way to an escape with his
Colt .45 pistol. He was killed.

During the Saint-Mihiel campaign, more
than eight hundred American pilots flew
overhead, taking photographs of troop
movements, strafing trenches, and dropping
bombs. Thirty-seven-year-old Colonel Billy
Mitchell, later general, commanded this force.
Mitchell insisted that massed air power could
destroy the enemy's will to fight. By the end of
the war, 45 American squadrons, totaling some
740 planes, were flying at the front. American
pilots shot down a total of 776 enemy aircraft
while losing only 289.

5

THE ELEVENTH HOUR

EVERYBODY WENT MAD. THE MEN RUSHED OUT OF THE TENTS AND SHOUTED: "IT'S OVER— IT'S OVER—IT'S OVER!" I COULD HEAR ONE SHRILL VOICE SCREAMING WILDLY: "NO MORE BOMBS—NO MORE SHELLS—NO MORE MISERY!"

—British private F. A. Voigt

Newspaper reporters crowded
around President Woodrow Wilson. He would
have to do "some plain talking when we get
on the other side," he told them. No president
ever before had left the United States while in
office. In December 1918, Wilson stood on the
deck of the U.S. troop ship *George Washington*
as it crossed the Atlantic Ocean on its way
to France.

A year earlier, Wilson had revealed his
thoughts on what a final peace treaty should
include. His "Fourteen Points" provided for free-
dom of the seas, smaller national armed forces,
new boundaries for some countries, and the inde-
pendence of Poland. It also called for a "League
of Nations," a general association of nations
whose goal would be to preserve world peace.

On December 13, the *George Washington* docked at the French port of Brest. A crowd of people cheered and saluted the arrival of the American president. Soon, a special train carried Wilson across the French countryside to Paris.

The war had killed millions of soldiers and sailors. More than 53,000 Americans had died in battle, another 63,000 of disease. That was a small number compared with the terrible cost to other nations. The British lost more than 900,000 in battle dead. Battlefield graves held the bodies of more than 1.3 million Frenchmen. Germany sacrificed the lives of about 1.75 million troops and Austria-Hungary about 1.2 million. Italy lost 650,000 soldiers, and Turkey mourned the loss of 300,000 troops. Russia suffered worse than any other nation, easily more than 4 million soldiers dead or missing. In addition, all across Europe, millions of civilians—men, women, and children—had died of hunger and disease.

Delegates representing twenty-seven nations gathered in Paris in January 1918. It was their duty to provide for a "just and lasting peace," as Wilson declared. As talks progressed, four people: President Wilson, British prime minister David Lloyd George, French prime minister Georges Clemenceau, and Italian prime minister Vittorio Orlando became the most important leaders. They became known as "the Big Four."

The Big Four spent hours studying maps. They decided upon fair borders for Europe's nations.

The Big Four sit for a photo during their peace meetings in Paris. From left to right are Vittorio Orlando, David Lloyd George, Georges Clemenceau, and Woodrow Wilson.

Three nations—Austria-Hungary, Montenegro, and Serbia—disappeared from the map of Europe. Nine new, independent countries came into existence: Latvia, Lithuania, Estonia, Poland, Czechoslovakia, Yugoslavia, Austria, Hungary, and Finland.

Delegates stepped forward and signed the final peace treaty in the Hall of Mirrors at Versailles, France, on June 28, 1919. In Paris, car horns blared, bands marched in parade, cannons boomed, and huge crowds cheered. The treaty heavily punished Germany. Article 231 forced Germany and her allies to admit guilt for starting the war. Article 232 demanded that Germany pay for all the damage done to the people and property of the Allies during the fighting. Germany lost control of its Rhineland and Saar

Valley regions for a period of fifteen years. The disputed provinces of Alsace and Lorraine were taken back by France.

When President Wilson returned from France, he called upon the U.S. Senate to ratify the Treaty of Versailles. "Dare we reject it and break the heart of the world?" he declared. He was shocked to learn, however, that many senators were against the treaty. As isolationists, they wished to keep the United States out of world affairs. They vowed to stop the United States from joining the League of Nations.

On September 3, 1919, Wilson began a national tour to fight for the treaty. His train stopped in twenty-nine cities, and he made dozens of speeches. Wherever the train stopped, cheering crowds pressed about his railroad car to see and hear him. In a month, the train covered eight thousand miles. But the strain proved too much for the president. While traveling from Pueblo, Colorado, to Wichita, Kansas, Wilson suffered a stroke. For months, he lay gravely ill. The health of his body and his mind were ruined, even though he would live another four years. On November 19, 1919, the Senate rejected the Versailles treaty. The League of Nations had been designed to save the world from future war, but the United States refused to join it.

Most of the doughboys in France had no interest in politics and diplomacy. They only wanted to return home. Sergeant Tom Brady remembered when his troop ship docked at Pier 54 in New York City in April 1919. "People working in the big office buildings waved flags and threw out ticker tape," he later wrote. "Red Cross nurses lined the pier and a Marine band played 'There Will Be a Hot Time . . . ,' 'How Dry I Am,' and other old songs, and the boys yelled themselves hoarse." Soldiers proudly marched in the streets before receiving their discharge papers and returning home.

After World War I ended, many of Europe's nations had new borders drawn. Nine new, independent nations were created and three countries disappeared from the European map. This is a map of Europe's new borders in 1919.

These troops had seen and done much during their time in Europe. They had changed a great deal and so had the nation. After the horrible experience of world war, Americans wanted to live it up. In 1919, the Eighteenth Amendment became part of the U.S. Constitution. This amendment outlawed the manufacture, sale, and transportation of alcoholic beverages.

Many people disobeyed this law. Gangsters, such as Al "Scarface" Capone and Charles "Lucky" Luciano, smuggled liquor into the country. Some people drank at illegal private clubs called "speakeasies" or mixed up batches of homemade gin in their bathtubs.

The lives of women in America greatly changed. In 1920, the Nineteenth Amendment to the Constitution was passed. It granted women the right to vote. "The victory is not a victory for women alone," exclaimed the *Kansas City Star*, "it is a victory for democracy and the principle of equality. . . . "[1] More and more women escaped their homes and joined the American workforce. Many joined the growing excitement of "the Roaring Twenties." The 1920s were a time of great change. Modern young women called themselves "flappers." They "bobbed" their hair by cutting it short, raised the hemlines of their dresses above the knee, and danced to the latest music—jazz.

Americans bought automobiles, including Henry Ford's cheap and popular Model T, "the Tin Lizzie." Free of their simple home lives, Americans traveled where and when they liked. On November 2, 1920, KDKA in Pittsburgh, Pennsylvania, became the world's first radio station. As other stations began broadcasting, Americans across the nation bought radios and enjoyed the latest news and entertainment.

Events in Europe also held the attention of Americans. In Russia, the Bolsheviks murdered Czar Nicholas II and his family. Several years of civil war shook Russia, as Vladimir Lenin struggled to create the Union of Soviet Socialist Republics (USSR). When Lenin died in 1924,

President Barack Obama visits Arlington National Cemetery on November 11, 2009, Veterans Day, to honor veterans of the wars in Iraq and Afghanistan. President Woodrow Wilson first declared November 11 a national holiday after the Germans signed the armistice ending World War I. It was known as Armistice Day until June 1, 1954, when Congress voted to change the holiday's name to Veterans Day, which it has been known as ever since.

Joseph Stalin grabbed control as Russia's dictator. Stalin brought harsh Communist rule to Europe's largest nation.

The Treaty of Versailles wrecked the economy of Germany. As the German government tried to pay war damages, the value of the German mark dropped shockingly. By the end of 1923, it took 4.2 trillion marks to equal one U.S. dollar. Germans loaded up wheelbarrows with stacks of their worthless money in order to buy a cup of coffee. A World War I corporal named Adolf Hitler rose to the leadership of the Nazi Party. In fiery speeches, Hitler preached German pride, race hatred, and revolution. By 1933, Hitler had become chancellor of Germany. His insane dreams of world conquest would lead to the start of World War II in 1939.

The United States joined this latest war in 1941. Veterans of World War I sadly watched their children march off to fight. The cruel lessons of war would have to be learned again. The hope and courage of Americans, however, remained the same. Woodrow Wilson had remarked after World War I, "The Americans who went to Europe to die are a unique breed. Never before have men crossed the seas to a foreign land to fight for a cause which they did not pretend was peculiarly their own, which they knew was the cause of humanity and mankind. These Americans gave the greatest of gifts, the gift of life and the gift of spirit."

Chronology

1914

June 28: Archduke Franz Ferdinand of Austria-Hungary is assassinated at Sarajevo by Serbian nationalist Gavrilo Princip.

July 28: Austria-Hungary declares war on Serbia.

August 1–3: Germany declares war on Russia and France; World War I begins.

August 29: Russian Army is defeated by German general Paul von Hindenburg at the Battle of Tannenberg.

September 14: German troops advance into France and are stopped at first battle of the Marne; trench warfare begins.

1915

May 7: A German submarine sinks the British liner *Lusitania*.

1916

January: British troops evacuate Turkey's Gallipoli Peninsula after failing to capture it.

February–June: Battle for Verdun, France.

May 31: Naval Battle of Jutland in the North Sea.

July–November: Battle of the Somme.

1917

March 16: Russian czar Nicholas II abdicates; provisional government takes over Russia.

April 6: The United States declares war on Germany.

November 7: The Bolshevik Revolution brings Socialist Vladimir Lenin to power in Russia.

December 9: British general Sir Edmund Allenby captures Jerusalem.

1918

March 3: Russians sign the Treaty of Brest Litovsk and drop out of the war.

March 21: Germans begin Operation Michael, their last offensive in France.

May 31: American troops arrive at Chateau-Thierry near Belleau Wood.

June 1: The American Second Division begins fight for Belleau Wood.

July–August: The Allies put Germany on the defensive during second battle of the Marne.

September 12–14: The Americans capture Saint-Mihiel salient.

September 26: The Americans begin attack in the Meuse-Argonne.

November 9: Germany collapses in revolution; Kaiser Wilhelm II abdicates his throne and flees the country.

November 11: Germans sign armistice at 5:30 A.M. at Compiegne, France; fighting ends at 11:00 A.M.

1919

June 28: World leaders sign the Treaty of Versailles, which officially ends the war.

Chapter Notes

1 THE SINKING OF THE *LUSITANIA*

1. D. Hickey and G. Hall, *Seven Days to Disaster* (New York: G. P. Putnam's Sons, 1982), p. 182.
2. Walter Millis, *Road to War: America 1914–1917* (New York: Howard Fertig, 1970), p. 164.
3. Charles Callan Tansill, *America Goes to War* (Gloucester, Mass.: Peter Smith, 1963), p. 290.
4. Louis Filler, ed., *The President Speaks* (New York: G. P. Putnam's Sons, 1964), p. 108.

2 THE WORLD AT WAR

1. Henry Berry, *Make the Kaiser Dance* (New York: Arbor House, 1978), p. 121.
2. Lyn Macdonald, *1914–1918: Voices & Images of the Great War* (London: Michael Joseph, Ltd., 1988), p. 19.
3. S.L.A. Marshall, *World War I* (Boston: Houghton Mifflin Company, 1964), p. 222.
4. Ibid.
5. Macdonald, p. 99.
6. Ibid., p. 155.
7. Marshall, p. 287.
8. Ibid., p. 333.

3 THE YANKS ARE COMING

1. William A. DeGregorio, *The Complete Book of U.S. Presidents* (New York: Dember Books, 1984), p. 424.
2. General George C. Kenney, "A Flier's Journal," *American Heritage* (December 1969), p. 46.
3. Edward M. Coffman, *The War to End All Wars* (Madison, Wis.: The University of Wisconsin Press, 1986), p. 15.
4. Editors of the *Army Times, The Yanks Are Coming* (New York: G. P. Putnam's Sons, 1960), p. 62.

5. A.J.P. Taylor, *The First World War* (Middlesex, England: Penguin Books, Ltd., 1963), p. 180.

6. Henry Berry, *Make the Kaiser Dance* (New York: Arbor House, 1978), p. 33.

4 RENDEZVOUS WITH DEATH

1. Bernard J. Gallagher, "A Yank in the B.E.F.," *American Heritage* (June 1965), p. 101.

2. Editors of the *Army Times, The Yanks Are Coming* (New York: G. P. Putnam's Sons, 1960), pp. 91–93.

3. Elton Mackin, "Suddenly We Didn't Want to Die," *American Heritage* (February/March 1980), p. 53.

4. Edward M. Coffman, *The War to End All Wars* (Madison, Wis.: University of Wisconsin Press, 1986), p. 237.

5. Henry Berry, *Make the Kaiser Dance* (New York: Arbor House, 1978), p. 188.

6. Captain Edward V. Rickenbacker, "Fighting the Flying Circus," *The Last Magnificent War* (New York: Paragon House, 1989), pp. 239–240.

5 THE ELEVENTH HOUR

1. S.L.A. Marshall, *World War I* (Boston: Houghton Mifflin Company, 1964), p. 429.

2. Laurence Stallings, *The Doughboys* (New York: Harper & Row Publishers, 1963), pp. 239–240.

3. Joe McCarthy, "The Lost Battalion," *American Heritage* (October 1977), p. 90.

4. Edward M. Coffman, *The War to End All Wars* (Madison, Wis.: University of Wisconsin Press, 1986), p. 324.

5. Captain Edward V. Rickenbacker, *"Fighting the Flying Circus," The Last Magnificent War* (New York: Paragon House, 1989), p. 251.

6 THE AFTERMATH

1. Sharon M. Himsl, ed., *1920–1940 The Twentieth Century* (San Diego: Greenhaven Press, 2004), p. 26.

Glossary

abdicate—To relinquish or give up power.

doughboys—A slang term for an American infantryman, most widely used during World War I.

dreadnought—A twentieth-century battleship.

dugout—In World War I, an area in the side of a trench used for living quarters, storage, or protection.

foxhole—A pit dug quickly for individual cover from enemy fire.

imperialist—An imperial government, such as France and Great Britain during World War I, which extends its power and dominion by acquiring and controlling other territories.

mortar—A muzzle-loading, high-angle gun with a short barrel that fires shells at high elevations for a short range.

mustard gas—A toxic gas used during World War I that causes blisters and attacks the eyes and lungs.

propaganda—Information or ideas that are spread to promote some cause or damage to another's cause.

shell shock—A mental disorder caused by the stress of active warfare.

starboard—The right side of a ship or aircraft.

stevedore—A worker who loads and unloads ships in a port.

U-boat—*Unterseeboot* (undersea boat), a German submarine.

zeppelin—A rigid type of German airship first used in the early twentieth century.

Further Reading

Books

Batten, Jack. *The War to End All Wars: The Story of WWI*. Toronto: Tundra Books, 2009.

Beller, Susan Provost. *The Doughboys Over There: Soldiering in World War I*. Minneapolis, Minn.: Twenty-First Century Books, 2008.

Freedman, Russell. *The War to End All Wars: World War I*. Boston: Clarion Books, 2010.

Langley, Andrew. *The Hundred Days Offensive: The Allies Push to Win World War I*. Minneapolis, Minn.: Compass Point Books, 2008.

Meyers, Walter Dean, and William Miles. *The Harlem Hellfighters: When Pride Met Courage*. New York: HarperCollins, 2006.

Murphy, Jim. *Truce: The Day the Soldiers Stopped Fighting*. New York: Scholastic Press, 2009.

Internet Addresses

Eyewitness to History.com: World War I
    <http://www.eyewitnesstohistory.com/w1frm.htm>

First World War.com:
    A Multimedia History of World War One
    <http://www.firstworldwar.com/index.htm>

PBS: The Great War
    <http://www.pbs.org/greatwar/>

Index